One day
they will tell stories of her.
About the girl
who walked through fire,
dined with the devil,
and then walked away.
With purpose in her footsteps
and confidence in her grin
she looked Satan in the face
and politely said -
hell is boring,
and I have shit to do.

Girl, don't let what you're going through stop you.
You have shit to do!

First paperback edition October 2022

Illustrated by Yvette Gilbert
Edited by Bianca Bowers

ISBN 979-8-218-07238-4

Published by Taylor Noel Horst

SHE

WILL

RISE

Taylor Noel Horst

To My Dad

I promise I will never stop rising.

To My Mom

Thank you for being my hero.

To Every Woman

You can rise. You will rise. You must rise. And when you do, pull others up with you.

THIS IS *MY* STORY.

THIS IS *YOUR* STORY.

THIS IS *OUR* STORY.

Contents

SHE

WILL

RISE

SHE IS ME.

SHE IS YOU.

SHE IS ALL OF US.

Who is *SHE*?

SHE is me. *SHE* is you. *SHE* is all of us. *SHE* is the woman you are, the woman you want to be, and the woman you are becoming. And this is our story and our testament. It is our hero's journey - our fall, our rise, our glorious comeback.

As we walk our hero's journey, we must make a choice: *will we become more of who the world thinks we should be, or more of who we are?*

Life is messy, and we all struggle at times to figure out who we are, who we are not, and who we want to be. But *SHE* is already within us. *SHE* is the person we can all become.

But to become *SHE*, we must confront, cry, question, uncover, and feel. We must courageously summon her and wake her from her sleep. *SHE* is there, and *SHE* is ready. The better question is, are you ready?

SHE FELL

We All Fall in Life.

Most of the time, these "falls" are small. We bounce back with minor cuts, bruises, and stories that start with, "this one time when."

But other times, at least once in our lifetime, we experience a fall so big and devastating that it's life changing.

We find ourselves broken, lying on the ground wondering, "how did I get here?" We feel lost, alone, and hopeless.

The fire that once burned inside us has turned to ash.

We have forgotten who we are and what we live for.

I have been there.
You have been there.
Perhaps, you are there right now.

when she's alone
she prays
to be somebody
else
because she isn't
good enough
pretty enough
or smart enough
she isn't
who she's supposed to be
or so she believes
so she cries
into her sheets every night
and she prays
that maybe one day
she will finally be
enough

You have always been enough,

and you always will be.

she looks back
to happier times
hoping they will remind her
what it was like
to be more than
"just fine."

she dreams of a place
she's never been
a world far different
from the one
she lives in

she's trapped
in a body
    she doesn't belong
in a life
    that isn't hers
in a world
    where nobody cares

You are not a ghost.

You are seen.

I promise that somebody sees you.

she leaned forward
and peered into the mirror
not to see
what she looked like
but to see
who was really there

there
in the mirror
she was too blind
to recognize
the beauty
of her own reflection

she belonged nowhere,
even her thoughts
rejected her

Our mind is the one space that we have absolute control over. If we do not first belong to ourselves, where will we ever belong.

when she sleeps
she is freed
from the nightmare
that is her reality

You live in what you create.

she's suffering inside
but nobody sees
so she puts up her walls
and lets the pain be

Sometimes, the protective walls we work so hard to build hurt us more because they keep the dark in and prevent the light from coming through.

who is she?
she only knows
who she's been told
she needs to be
to live a life
that pleases everybody

Don't lose yourself in who "they" think you should be.

she's afraid she'll never know
a life of love.
is it something
she is even capable of?
for her heart is one
of her broken parts,
and how could she feel love
when she can't feel
much at all?

Love starts inside. It comes from the inside first.

in life's eyes
what was she,
besides another human
being?
a speck of sand
on an ocean beach
too tiny
to compare,
too fragile
to exist
anywhere.

she had a tendency
to ruin good things
before they even began

Don't overthink things into existence.

masks.
they cover up what she feels inside,
not that she's proud,
but she's a very good liar.
you will only see what she shows you,
and she can make you believe
that she is anybody.
she wears these masks
because she's scared.
if she takes them off,
will you like who is really there?

she's slipping
she's falling
she's fading away
into a black hole
that she made

Our prisons, we build them ourselves.

she's a loner
she's shy
when she's by herself
all she does is cry
she hides her sorrows
behind a smile
but she's not happy
hasn't been for a while
she wonders if there's more to life
if not
she'd rather just die

Don't ever wish yourself away. The pain that accompanies living, is never greater than the gift of being alive.

she's lost
in an abyss
of unawareness
and she's drowning
in a sea of sameness
slowly losing
the never-ending battle
to keep breathing
to keep her head
above water

Fight.

Even when you feel like you can't any longer,

fight to keep breathing.

she's trying so hard
to isolate herself
from the enemy
but somehow
she can't escape
herself

Our shadows

will always chase us

until we find the courage

to face them.

everyday
she wore a lie
to hide her truth-
I want to die.

You don't have to hide it. Give your pain a voice.

why does she smile
when she really wants to cry?
why does she laugh
when she only feels hurt inside?
why does she keep fighting
when she really wants to quit –
to surrender to the dark voices
and just give in?

Why? Because joy and happiness exist, and you can achieve them.

it's been a while
since she smiled,
laughed,
or even cared.
she can't help but wonder,
why she is even here.

You are here because you are meant to be here. The Universe doesn't make mistakes.

she's playing
Russian Roulette
with death,
never knowing
when she might take
her last breath.

she's fighting a war
that's leaving her bloodied and bruised,
the battles are never ending
and she's not bullet proof.
the wars are taking their toll,
she's at a crossroads
and it's time to choose –
is life a cause
worth fighting for,
or is it time
to raise the white flag
and lose?

I know it hurts. Life puts us through so many battles. We encounter rocky roads and have to make difficult choices. But when the time comes and you must choose, I hope you choose the difficult path that leads to uncovering more of the real you.

she doesn't know
how long
the band-aids will hold
her bullet holes.

nothing
but a blank stare
from the overwhelming
misery and despair
trapped within
so cold and numb
it's paralyzing
the only way to cope
is to feel
absolutely
nothing

in a pool
of her own blood
is where she lies
with tears
streaming down her face,
a bottle of Jack
to numb the pain,
and a sharpened blade
to bleed from her veins
every ounce of impurity
every trace of pain.

cold
cold and numb
cold, numb, and afraid.
she's afraid
she's terrified
of herself
of what she's done
of who she has become.
her hands are stained red
from her blood.
what has she done?

How Do We "lose" Ourselves?

If we are born pure, how do we become impure? If we are born whole, why do we feel as though we are broken? If, when we enter this world, we are connected, how do we become so distant?

Losing our connection to who we really are is the essence of the fall. It's the gradual decline of our own self-awareness.

As children, we are vibrant and full of life. Where does that spirit go as we get older? How do we go from possessing an absolute love for life to thinking of life as a chore?

I don't know that we will ever be able to pinpoint the exact time in our lives when we started our downfall and began to lose connection with our inner selves. Unfortunately, because of the nature of our society, our fall begins from the moment we are born.

The signs are subtle, but they are there – the voice in the back of our head and the feeling inside our gut. Our obsession with the material world causes us to neglect our inner world. Our desires to be accepted and loved by everyone move us further away from accepting and loving ourselves. We get lost in the masks and the lies, and we soon discover that our true face is nowhere in sight. The question of, "who do I need to be to be loved and accepted by others" becomes more important than, "who do I need to be so that I love and accept myself?"

It's quite the paradox. According to the laws of human nature, by default, we are beings of love, self-acceptance, and authenticity. Why then are those the very things we are always trying to find?

Why is the hardest fight, learning to love ourselves?

Why is our worst enemy, our reflection?

Why do we put being accepted by others ahead of accepting ourselves?

There are so many questions to be answered and so many truths to be found. But perhaps the most puzzling question of all is, "what is it about the journey through the dark that enables us to discover our light?

Concealed Underneath

The journey through the dark, if we allow it, can be one of the most important and enlightening processes we can experience. When we walk through the dark, we discover and return to our light. It is the journey that allows us to return to our true home – our internal home. Through our experience with darkness, we see how our true selves have been concealed from years of damage and conditioning.

By exploring our darkest depths, we find that our most valuable treasure is ourselves. The "self" that we see glimpses of every now and then and ask, "where did *SHE* go?" But SHE never went anywhere. *SHE* is still there, *SHE* always has been. *SHE'S* just sleeping, like sleeping beauty, waiting for that kiss from her prince. That "prince" is the dark. Being kissed by the darkness wakes up the warrior that resides within you. And when *SHE*, *you*, wakes, you find yourself at perhaps the biggest life-turning point you will ever encounter.

Turning Points

At some moment in our life, we reach a turning point. It is from here that our lives go one of two ways, towards enlightenment or oblivion. Which way we go, I believe, comes down to our character and our will to both survive and thrive.

We all experience these turning points differently, yet similarly in the fact that they are terrifying. How we navigate these critical turning points writes our future. Either we write in our life story that we chose to climb the mountains, walk through hell, and fight our demons, or we write nothing, because our story ended, either physically, mentally, or both.

But it has been my observation and experience that we write in our story that we chose to claw, scream, cry, and do whatever it took. Why? Because the warrior within refuses to let her story end in the dark.

Your story isn't over.

SHE CRIED

The Healing Process

What is healed? What does it look like? Above all, what does "healed" feel like?

As I have walked my path towards being "healed", I have pondered these questions and discovered that viewing "being healed" as a destination is elusive, misleading, and daunting. It is also nearly impossible to define what it looks and feels like.

Instead of defining healing as an emotion, I choose to define it as an action. I define the act of healing as having courage. Choosing healing, just like choosing courage, is choosing to be brave even when we are scared. Healing is a messy and scary process, which is why we must act courageously as we walk along its path.

I break the healing process into four parts – the 4 C's. According to the 4 C's, the path of healing consists of:

1. Contemplating
2. Confronting
3. Crying, and
4. Courage.

Contemplating

Before we begin to walk the healing path, we contemplate if it is something we want to do. We fear the process of healing, but we are also afraid of being healed. Being healed hints at the prospects of happiness, love, and peace. Those things are scary when you have only ever been broken, lost, and barely hanging on.

Just the thought of experiencing something new, that could feel good, requires us to stop and think if we are willing to do what it takes to get there. Moving towards healing means moving away from whatever has broken us. It means walking into unfamiliar territory and uncomfortable experiences, which we are biologically wired to want to avoid. We want safe, and what we know is safe, even if what we know isn't what we want.

Confronting

Once we decide that we are interested, but not fully vested in, walking the healing path, we move into the confronting stage. Here, we begin to examine ourselves by traveling into our past and revisiting situations and experiences that we believe helped to shape us. We do this to figure out why we are the way we are. Why did I make the choices that led to a certain outcome? Is who I am genuinely who I want to be?

For the first time, we stare into the depths of our reflection. If our reflection aligns with who we believe ourselves to be, we continue walking the path we are one. But, if who we see is not who we believe ourselves to be, or is not the person we want to be, we must make a choice. Either we choose to live in incongruence, or we take full responsibility for the choices we have made, the things we have done, and the person we have become. We also recognize that it is our responsibility to do the necessary work to live a life where we are in congruence.

Crying

If we truly confront our reflection and honestly evaluate who we are in the confrontation stage, the feelings of guilt, regret, and sadness can overwhelm to the point that we enter the "crying" stage.

We cry because we are angry, sad, and confused. Though eventually, we cry because it feels good to cry. We finally recognize that crying is what we need to do because it is something we haven't allowed ourselves to do. We need to cry. We need to grieve past versions of us that no longer serve us. Crying and grieving cleanses the soul and gives us a clean slate; the opportunity to begin again.

Courage

Courage isn't the last stage of the healing process, it's actually the beginning. Going through the previous stages brings us to the point where we can no longer live as we are, as someone we are not meant to be. This realization is what brings us to the "courage" stage and the point where we can begin walking the healing path. This is when we become vested in the process. It's no longer a question of if we want to be healed, it is something that we must do.

Finding the Courage to Take the Leap

It is not our rise from the dark that promotes our healing, it's our healing that allows us to ascend out of the dark. In the dark is where we learn to surrender to that tiny flicker of light that resides within us. In the dark is where we learn to feel again. Learning to feel is a big part of healing, perhaps the most important part. In fact, part of walking the healing path is learning to become comfortable with how uncomfortable feeling makes us feel.

When we sit in the dark long enough, the unfamiliar begins to become familiar. Our eyes slowly adjust, our other senses heighten, and our intuition strengthens. Once we adjust, the magic begins.

When the darkness becomes familiar enough to see every demon that surrounds us and every obstacle that prevents us from coming home, that is when we give ourselves the opportunity to face the truth. Because, for the first time, we can see the truth.

It's time to hurt. It's time to cry. It's time to feel. It's time to find the courage to heal.

she's dying to live
but,
she's scared to death.

*At what point do we reach and cross the threshold of
fear and risk, and simply take the leap?*

deliverance,
is what she needs.
sweet deliverance,
she needs to be freed.
from her chains,
from herself.
she needs deliverance
from this hell.

We are both the captor of our freedom, and the giver
of our relief.

can she ever
redeem
the person
she used to be?

Asking for redemption only hinders our ability to move forward. Redemption is granted by becoming the person we were created to be. Stop looking back at who you were and start looking forward to who you are becoming.

she fought back the tears
while battling her fears.
but if only she knew
that the tears from her eyes
were part of her battle cry,
composted of holy water
to easer her pain
and rebirth her again

she's stuck somewhere between
where she's been
and where she's going.
she's confused
and conflicted.
her heart wants something,
but her mind
is caught up
in the not knowing.

*Only through walking into the unknown can we
make what is there known. Through experiencing the
unfamiliar, we make it familiar.*

she's homesick
not for a place,
but for a feeling
for feeling
like herself.

she decided,
*it's time to be
brave.*

*One decision can change the course of your
entire life.*

she always kept her promises
to all,
except herself.

It's

time

to

honor

you.

let it rain
fire from above
and burn away
all she's not
so she can be
who she was destined
to become.

The Purpose of Our Tears

Tears are magical because they possess so much healing power. Crying opens the flood gates and lets the pain spill from our veins.

Our tears are pure, composed of holy water to help cleanse from our souls everything that no longer serves us. When we cry, we release all the hate, shame, and pain that kills our inner selves, and we water the seeds that grow true and lasting change.

If our tears cleanse, why are we so afraid to cry? Is it because crying is associated with feeling pain, and we don't want to feel pain? But to return home, we need to feel the pain. We must kill habits, behavior patterns, thought processes, and versions of ourselves that have been part of us but no longer serve us.

Crying brings us face to face with the truth of the dark. The dark is where we unmask our demons and discover that it is our face we see. The truth of the dark is that we are the demons that have been stalking us. We are our lies, false identities, self-betrayals, and past mistakes.

Sitting with our pain is frightening. Crying is exhausting. But it must be that way. We cannot run and learn at the same time. The truth is unveiled in the silence. Only when we stop running and allow our shadows to catch up with us can we finally examine all that we cling to, and all that keeps us trapped.

she cried
because her eyes
could no longer hide
the flood
that lay behind

Cry a river,

build a raft with your broken pieces

and float down the river of self-discovery.

her tears
created a river
that allowed her to float
towards a future
bearing a fresh canvas
where she could paint
from a heart-centered space
the life
she yearned to find

realization hit her like a train.
hate
guilt
and shame
had caused all her pain.
she had to release it
only forgiveness led to growth.

she tore down her walls
and released the pain.
carrying her burdens
would prevent her
from becoming
who she wanted to be.

she chose to feel again
even though feeling
hurt the most.
if she wanted to feel love
she had to learn
to feel the pain.

*Love and pain go hand in hand. You can't have one
without the other.*

she made peace
with the monsters
inside her head
and declared
darkness
her friend.

she discovered that despite
the heartache and pain
love and happiness
can still reign.

she finally stood
dismantled
completely naked
on the precipice of relearning
herself
for the very first time

Entering the Cocoon

Caterpillars are not meant to stay caterpillars forever. They are meant to change into butterflies. But what happens before they can change? They must build a cocoon, inside which they are alone and isolated. Their old body needs to be broken down and turned into something completely new. Caterpillars don't magically morph into butterflies. They are created a butterfly from the ruins of what they used to be.

We must do the same. We were not created to be depressed, anxious, fearful, or unworthy. We were created to be beautiful creatures with wings. We are destined to fly – to be happy and full of life. But to get there, we must build a cocoon and explore the deepest, darkest depths of ourselves. We must break down and strip away every single layer of who we think we are.

she was a caterpillar
hungry for change
so, she built a cocoon
and there she stayed
in the quiet
and in the dark
until she found
a tiny spark
within her soul
that she nurtured
into a flame and
then a fire
that burned the cocoon away
and from the inferno
she emerged
completely changed
with a pair of wings
to fly away

Breaking Free

Our time to emerge from the cocoon comes with the realization and acceptance that we were never designed to be grounded. Once we understand that we were created to fly, and that our ability to do so has always been within us, it is time to break free from the cocoon – to begin our rise out of the dark.

The moment we break free is the moment we stop shedding tears. It's the moment when we stop looking down and finally look up. We gaze at the sky with a fierce determination that was previously missing. Our newfound fierceness creates an insatiable desire to use our wings to ascend out the dark towards heights we only ever dreamed of.

Your story isn't over.

SHE
Decided R I S E
To

Why We Rise

We *RISE* because we were not born to live grounded.

We *RISE* because defeat is not our default, and it is certainly not our destiny.

We *RISE* because, although we feel lost at times, we absolutely know who we are and what we are capable of.

We *RISE* because of the fire, the pull, and the desire to persist, so that we can be, do, create, and truly live.

We *RISE* because we are warriors. We *RISE* because our story doesn't end in the dark.

from the ashes,
she did not pick up her remains
instead,
she buried them

she finally found
someone worth
fighting for –
herself.

*YOU. The most important person you will ever fight
for.*

she couldn't rebuild
on a foundation of lies
that is how
she crumbled
the first time.

Going back to the way "you used to be" is a decision unworthy of the new you. You can't become who you want to be by remaining who you were. <u>Build your new empire on the foundation of your truth</u>.

her faith gave her wings
but hope
allowed her to fly

Faith is trust. To have faith means to trust that, even though you don't understand why something is happening, it is happening for a reason. Faith gives us wings because, although we face uncertainty, we trust that our wings will be there to catch us.

Hope is belief. To have hope means to believe that you will find what you are looking for, even if it seems as though it is nowhere to be found. Hope allows us to fly because it is our belief in a better future that allows us to achieve a better future.

no longer is she
the one who runs and hides
from her dreams
from her fears
from her reflection
in the mirror

she's fighting tired eyes
a tired body
and a tired mind
but fighting is easier
than taming the fire
of burning desire
that rages on
deep inside her

As long as the flame burns, you can keep going.

she walks through fire
like she's fireproof
but she's just not afraid
to burn

by walking through the fire
she earned a sword
stronger than steel
sharper than broken glass
this sword
she now wields
ready to slay her demons
ready to slay her foes
no longer is she afraid
of the path
she must walk alone

Nothing is scarier than being alone in the dark.

Nothing is as painful as completely dissecting yourself.

Nothing can be as enlightening as silence and as powerful as finding the courage to walk the path you must walk alone.

she killed them off
one by one
the people who hurt her
the places that robbed her
of her identity
the thoughts
that whispered she was unworthy
and the things
that stunted her growth
everything
that was holding her back
had to be let go

Separating from everything that once was is perhaps one of the hardest, yet most necessary, things you will ever do.

she didn't know
the road less traveled
would be so lonely

*The **RISE** isn't easy. The path of accepting yourself
is lonely. But you come to see that although you are
alone, you do not feel empty like you once did.*

a lion's roar
could not compare
to the voice she found
when she overcame her fear

she carried with her pieces
of whom she used to be
as a reminder
of where she came from
and why
she could never go back

*We will always carry with us parts of who we used to
be. Even though we no longer give those parts life-en-
ergy, they were still part of us at one point. Whether
good or bad, the parts of our past help connect the
dots of our future.*

Coming Home

For each of us, our inner "home" is unique. But I think that, despite the differences, it feels safe, warm, and above all, it feels right. When we come home, we return to a place of peace, love, and true acceptance. We walk the healing path in the hopes that it leads us back to that place within that feels like home. Home is what we desire most. it is what we ache for. And, eventually, it becomes what we will bare suffering for.

We try to find home in places, people, and things, but it doesn't exist in those places because "home" is a feeling. Home is a place within us that we must tune into. It's necessary to look for home in places where we won't find it because that is how we learn where it truly exists. Experiencing what feels wrong helps us to understand what feels right. That way, when we do come home, we know we are there.

I think that coming home is something that we must repeatedly do throughout our life journey. We are going to get lost and we are going to stray. That is part of the adventure of living and finding what is truly meant for us. We shouldn't fear getting lost because if we remain fearful, we will never take the risky leaps that are required for true self-discovery.

Perhaps the biggest mistake that we can make on the journey home is not making the journey at all. Coming home takes time. It's not a process that we can, nor should we want to, rush. We need to take our time and put in that deep, inner soul work.

In the end, those who seek, are those who find.

It's time to

come home.

she stood unwavering
against the howling winds
and skin-piercing rain
still
quiet
and unafraid
to face the storm
and the demons it would bring
because she knew
she had all the strength
she needed to prevail
already within

Be still, calm, and confident. Be courageous. Allow who you are to lead the way and the more you will become unafraid.

she will rise
a phoenix
from the ashes
a Valkyrie
from the battlefield
wearing a dress
made of hellfire
she will rise

Conquer this life as only you can.

she was destined to be
fierce
strong
and full of fire
an angel
with a golden halo
and wings
resilient enough
to withstand the fire

Recognize your own tenacity – your own ability to fight and prevail despite the odds.

she was designed for this –
the struggle
the fight,
the battles
the wars of life.
God made her a warrior,
how can she not
rise?

*After a while you realize that you wouldn't be who
you are without the struggle. You look back at all you
have been through in life and you see that through
the struggles, setbacks, and massive heartbreaks,
you were forged. You were designed to handle every-
thing you have been through and everything you will
continue to face.*

she's got a fire in her belly
and hunger in her eyes
nothing can stop her
she's too determined
to rise

she was not born a warrior
she was forged
like a blacksmith shapes a sword
by the heat of the fire
she too was shaped
through the flames
from the knives
by the bullets
from the path she's walked
she has been forged
and it has prepared her
for the untraveled road
that lies before her

*Life finds the most inconvenient ways to teach us the
most important lessons.*

she's not who
she used to be
she's changed
from the trauma she's endured
and what she's done
to set herself free

Don't be ashamed to do what you have to do, for you.

she wasn't perfect
and she wasn't broken
she was patched and sewn
like a quilted blanket
with thread made of
hope, faith, love
and fabric from
the people and experiences
that shaped her
into the woman
she had become

she's covered in scars
each one an "x"
that marks the spot
of a past wreck
a permanent symbol
that damage was done
yet a beautiful treasure
that signifies
the battle was won

Our scars are the maps of our lives – of who we are
and where we have been. Explore your wrecks. See
the damage that was done, but also see the treasure
that has prevailed. You. The amazing person you
have become.

behind her eyes
is a story you don't know
a story of struggle
a story of strength
the story of a girl
who decided
she was worth it

Your story is such a powerful thing. The story of how you struggled and still thrived could be the birthing ground that helps someone else rise. Don't be afraid of your story. It's the story of you.

she found a way to live
where she doesn't feel trapped
she found her light
she found her truth
she found what her soul
was meant to do

she refused
to dim her light
just because
it was too blinding
for some

Don't dim your light. There is no such thing as shining too bright.

she embraced
her different
and in doing so
she magnified
her beauty

Your different is what makes you beautiful. Embrace it.

she fell in love
with giving love
to others,
to life,
but most importantly,
to herself.

*Give more love to others when you don't think you
have any to give.
Give more love to life when you don't think it could be
any worse.
Give more love to yourself even when you think there
is nothing about you to love.*

she dreams with her eyes wide open
and she walks toward those dreams
with a fiery soul
a passionate heart
and an open hand
for those who wish to follow

*When we live our truth, we give those around us the
courage to live their truths. When we chase what sets
our souls on fire, we reach out an open hand that
says, "It's okay to come along."*

she's unbreakable
not because she can't be broken
but because she's been broken
so many times
she's learned to thrive
among the pieces

*You don't need to fit all the pieces back together. You
need to learn to thrive amidst your brokenness.*

she's not fearless
just very courageous
a quality she derived
from seeing the depths of hell
and walking through the fire
to save herself

she was born among mortals
and she'll die just the same
but behind her she'll leave
a legacy
that will forever cause ripples
in the hearts
of all humanity

and there she'll be
dancing
in the storm
thriving
in the chaos

One of the most beautiful things in life is learning to dance in the storm. Even when there is absolute madness happening all around you, learn to embrace the chaos. It's part of what makes life worth living.

how foolish was she
to ever think
she was not loved

*Even when you think it is not possible for even one
person to love you, you are wrong. You are deeply
loved by so many people. Always remember that.*

there
in the mirror
she saw the face
of a girl
of a woman
a warrior
that she had always known
lived inside her

Afterword

I wish I had all the right things to say to you. I wish, that as a writer, I could write your life a beautiful and peaceful story. I wish that I had the ability to write away your suffering and make your life journey that much easier and more joyful. But your story is not mine to write, it is yours. So, what I wish more is for you to see the power that lives within yourself. I think that as a writer, that is the greatest gift I can give.

You are made of matter. The same matter that makes up this universe. That means that you are this universe compacted into a singular unit. You possess within you the same power that the universe has.

Look around you. There is abundance, truth, love, and infinite possibility everywhere. Realize that all of that is also within you. You are powerful and your potential is infinite.

What do you do when you realize you hold that

much power? You write your story. Write it exactly the way that you want it to be. Don't sugar coat it or water it down so that it sounds okay and makes sense to others.

Write people out of and into your life. Write your story of struggle, triumph, love, and loss. Above all, write your story with a happy ending, your happy ending.

Also know that no matter what, you are going to be okay. You are going to be hurt and you're going to break, more than a few times. Even still, you're going to be okay.

There is going to come a point when you will question yourself and everything about life, but eventually you are going to figure it all out. I don't know the exact moment when, but you'll fit all the pieces together. It might be for the first time in ten years or the tenth time in just one year. It might be with glue, rope, thread, or whatever else you can find, but you will mend yourself. You will heal. You will feel whole again.

In the process of putting yourself back together, you will discover things you never knew about yourself and life. You'll throw out pieces that somehow made their way into your story even though they didn't belong. Your life, and everything you have been through, will begin to make sense. The beautiful thing about being broken is that you gain this sense of invincibility, you have put yourself back together for yourself, by yourself. You have gained the invaluable ability to persevere on your own.

Once you know that you can heal yourself, you're not so scared anymore. You know that no matter what, you can make it. You can put yourself back together again and again. Then, when you are ready, you'll share your story of how you made yourself whole and you will inspire those around you to do the same. They will then repeat the process, and eventually we will have an army of healed individuals who realize and embrace the power of their story and who they are. Can you imagine the type of world we could create?

And just one last thing I want to say...

There is no one like you. There never was anyone like you. There never will be, in the future of this world, anyone like you.

You are unique, special, and beautiful. You deserve and are worthy of love. Your pain is giving birth to new life and what you are going through is happening for you. In hindsight, you'll be able to look back and connect the dots. But until that day arrives, have faith that everything is going to be okay.

Have faith in the journey, but more importantly, have faith in yourself.

Give your pain a voice and give your fear a face.
End your suffering,
discover who you are,
and then...

RISE

WARRIOR

RISE!

she is the one
holding my hand
as I walk through the dark
she is my light
and my guardian
she is my everlasting strength
and my forever best friend

Listen to who you are. Trust that quiet voice in your head, those butterflies in your stomach, and that beat in your heart. Never lost sight of yourself. Follow your true north – it will always guide you to where you are supposed to be, to who you have always been.

and she became
who she always aspired to be
the woman
courageous enough to chase
and to live
her dreams

*Become the woman you need to become. Create your
life. Become the embodiment of who and what you
aspire to be.*

A Personal Note...

Why I wrote this book...

"I want to be known for my voice. For how I made people feel. For being relentless in the pursuit of what sets my soul on fire. For inspiring people to better themselves and create lives they love living."

This is my personal mission statement. It is written on a sticky not and posted to the wall in front of my desk. Every time I pick up my pencil, it reminds me that my voice is powerful.

Honestly, I have been afraid to write these words for the longest time. But I have this voice within, and it would not let me put my pencil down. I wrote this book because not doing so would have been the beginning of my insanity.

As this book started to take form and come to life, I realized that the price of not publishing made me more uncomfortable than the exposure it might bring. My path has forged me for this, and I understand now that I was created for this. I'm not scared anymore. I have fought for my life to help you fight for yours. I was given this gift of writing to share my struggle. I can't change your life for you, but perhaps I can help you view it in a new way.

I think that in our society depression is often viewed as a disability. It's viewed as this scary monster that we should be afraid, and ashamed, of facing. In the beginning, I did too. But as I sat in the dark alone, and I refused to be defeated, my perspective started to change. I began to see my depression as an opportunity instead of an obstacle. I turned my disability into an ability. My depression gave me the ability to go within myself.

Going within is a scary place to go, but it's the journey through the scary places that lead us back home. Had it not been for my depression, I would not be here today. I would not be living in the state of pure bliss that fills me with so much love, peace, and happiness. I wouldn't have found myself. And now that I fully accept and live as the most authentic version of me, I don't even want to imagine what my life would have been like had I not come home.

I want you to know that there is hope for you to. Even in the most dismal moments there is hope and that hope lives within you. You must only have the courage to go find it.

What to do with this book.

If you found hope and courage within these pages, I encourage you to share it with someone. I also invite you to share your story. Share it with me or with someone who has earned the right to honor your struggle with you.

Unfortunately, there are so many stigmas and labels in our world today, especially regarding mental health, which not only includes depression and anxiety, but also identity, sexuality, and so much more. And although I wish it weren't the case, I don't think we will ever be able to rid society of the stigmas and labels that surround these topics. I do believe, however, that we can bridge the gap.

We start to do that by becoming more vulnerable through the sharing of our unique stories. We can bring more awareness, and through doing so, we can bring more change. Through sharing our imperfections, we inspire others to realize they don't need to be perfect. Sharing is how we start the chain reaction, the ripple effect. It's how we bring the awareness that leads to change.

So, allow me to start...

My name is Taylor, and I don't struggle with depression and anxiety, I dance with them. It took me a lot of dance lessons before we became in-step, and sometimes we still step on each other's toes. But it is not the quality of the dance, it is choosing to learn how to.

You don't have to shout it to the world, but I encourage you to at least tell someone you love and trust. Letting people know that we are not okay, makes not being okay, okay. That's the type of world I want to live in.

We must face our own demons and then we must share our story so that we may help others face their demons. We must fight together. We must rise together. Find your worth and then help others find theirs!

When the dark comes knocking at your door, my hope is that you'll take out this book to remind you of who you really are.

It's time to Rise.

Share your story and use the hashtags *#shewillrise*
#iamshe #mystory
Let's create a world where we are not scared to share
our stories. A world where we are not ashamed to be
who we are.
A world where we do not let the dark be the place
where our story ends.

Don't forget how strong you are.

You matter.

Your story isn't over. It has only just begun.

E

S

It's Time To

I

R

Meet the Author

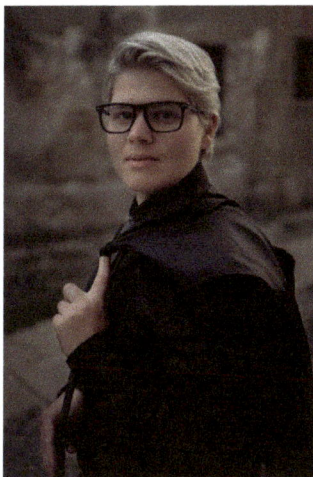

TAYLOR NOEL HORST grew up in a small town in Northeast Nebraska. She wrote her first poem in the 4th grade after her dog, and best friend, had to be euthanized. Since then, writing, especially poetry, has been an outlet, saving grace, and the thing that sets her soul on fire. She writes to heal, understand, and to teach and inspire. Through insurmountable adversity, Taylor has not just learned to survive, she has learned to thrive. In her debut poetry collection, *She Will Rise*, she speaks to the undeniable truth, that we can rise from anything. *She Will Rise* takes you on the journey of uncovering and defining the truth of yourself and the truth of life - you can fall, you can cry, and you can always ***decide to rise!***

Besides being a writer, Taylor is a Life Transformation Coach and Motivational Speaker. Her passion is helping people, especially women, realize their worth and become unstuck so that they can create and live lives they love as the best version of themselves.

Follow Taylor on Instragram @taylornoelhorst and
@taylornoel poetry. You can also visit
taylornoelofficial.com